MULTIPLY: Adventures at Prosperity Patch

by Kim D. H. Butler
and Spencer Shaw

MULTIPLY: Adventures at Prosperity Patch
Copyright © 2025 Kim D. H. Butler and Spencer Shaw

Prosperity Economics Movement
22790 Highway 259 South
Mount Enterprise, TX 75681
www.ProsperityEconomics.org

First Edition
ISBN: 979-8-9940994-5-2 (paperback)

Produced in the United States of America

Published with the assistance of Social Motion Publishing, which specializes in books that benefit causes and nonprofits. For more information, go to SocialMotionPublishing.com.

Acknowledgments

I love animals; I have had dogs, cats, chickens, pigs, sheep, goats, and dairy cows since 4th grade, and now I have Alpacas! I also love Prosperity Thinking. Now, I am excited to share these loves with children of all ages through my third love: reading! Whether you are an adult or have children, grandchildren, or great-grandchildren, reading with others (and playing games too!) is a fabulous bonding experience, and I am so grateful to the team of Spencer and family for bringing it to your table.

Enjoy, Kim Butler, Mount Enterprise, TX

I grew up hearing stories from my dad and kinfolk which shaped my world today. Sharing stories with kids is a fun way to help them think about big dreams. Huge thank you to my wife for leading our homeschooling and our kids for listening to these stories. A big thank you to Emma for helping Kim and I feel like children again.

We are so grateful to everyone who helps us make this book, like Amanda who leads this project and our awesome designers Cy and Holly.

Spencer Shaw

During a sunlit morning at Prosperity Patch, Emma, the wise Great Dane, gathered her friends around the big oak tree. "We have saved enough money to start a really big and exciting project," she announced. "Let's plant an orchard!"

The pets were thrilled at the idea, as they dreamed of an orchard filled with different types of fruit trees. "This orchard will not just give us delicious fruits," Emma explained,

"but it will also help us earn money, teach others, and host fun events."

The planning began. Miguel the strong bull took on the job of preparing the land.

Zippy the rabbit was in charge of getting the best seedlings.

Peanut the cat designed educational materials for visitors,

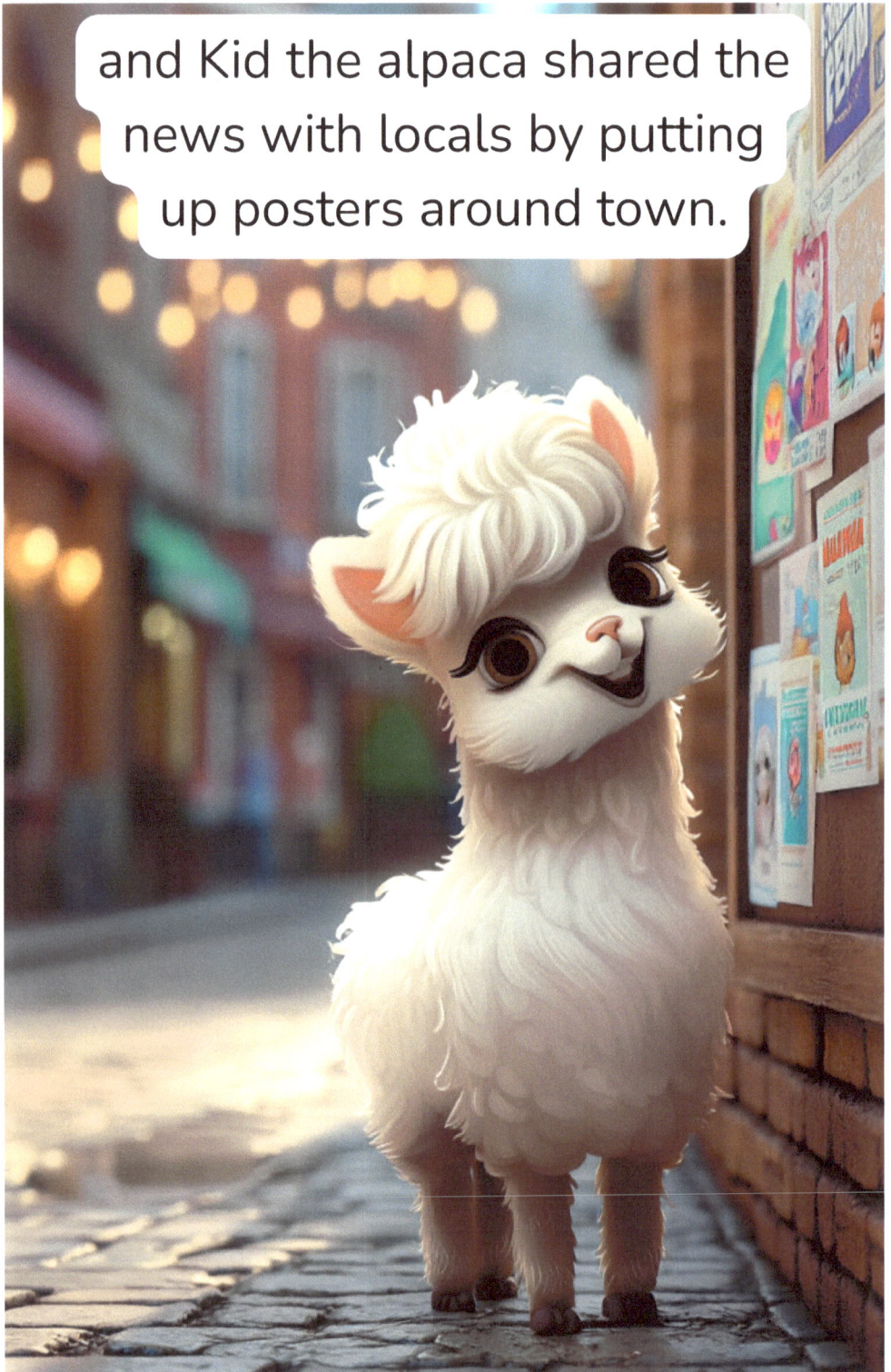

and Kid the alpaca shared the news with locals by putting up posters around town.

They invested in good tools and resources to make sure the orchard would grow strong and healthy.

As the plants grew, the pets watched their hard work start to pay off.

By the time the first fruits were ready, the pets used them to make delicious jams and pies.

They also started hosting school trips and offering tours for those who wanted to learn about farming sustainably.

Seeing how successful the orchard was, the pets decided to add more features.

They built a picnic area and a small shop where visitors could buy their jams, pies, and apple cider, donuts and slushies.

They even started a scholarship fund with some of the profits to help local students who were interested in agriculture. This way, their investment was helping to educate young people about farming.

As they looked around at all they had achieved, the pets felt proud.

The orchard had truly multiplied their money and done so much good for the community.

Sitting under the shade of a fruit-heavy tree, Emma shared, "This orchard shows us how smart investing can really make a difference.

Our money has helped us create a beautiful space, educate our friends, and give back to the community."

Emma's Advice:

Hey there, young thinker! Did you know your money can do more than one good thing at a time? Let's think about it like a magic coin. With it, you can help others and have fun too! You could use it to buy a toy you really like and also help a friend or cause.

It's like your magic coin is doing two good things at once! You can even save some to make your magic coin grow bigger over time. Remember, it's okay to ask for help from grown-ups or friends when you need a little extra magic. With practice, you'll be great at making your money do many wonderful things!

Emma's Questions:

1. What are some fun things you can make or do, that you could share with others?

2. Do you have toys or books you don't use anymore that you could sell or trade with friends to help buy something new or help someone else?

3. How could you use your time and talents to bring smiles to people in your neighborhood?

4. Can you think up a way to have fun while helping your family too?

5. What are some ways you could save the money you earn, to help buy something special or give to someone who needs it?

A note for your parents!

As our thank-you, the QR code below will give you a valuable white paper focused on Income Strategies at ProsperityEconomics.org/permission.